Was Lee A Traitor?

Robert E. Lee

Was Lee A Traitor?

Walter D. Kennedy

SHOTWELL
COLUMBIA · SO. CAR.
EST. 2015
PUBLISHING

Produced in the Republic of South Carolina by

SHOTWELL PUBLISHING LLC
Post Office Box 2592
Columbia, So. Carolina 29202

www.ShotwellPublishing.com

Cover: Portrait of Gen. Robert E. Lee, officer of the Confederate Army. United States, March 1864. Photograph by Vannerson, Julian. LOC.gov

Frontispiece: Robert E. Lee / Vic Arnold. , ca. 1882. N.Y.: A.S. Seer's Litho Print, 26 & 28 Union Square, June 22. Arnold, Vic, Artist. LOC.gov

ISBN: 978-1-963506-23-5

FIRST EDITION

10 9 8 7 6 5 4 3 2 1

CONTENTS

Chapter I

WHO WAS LEE AND
WHAT DIFFERENCE DOES IT MAKE?

I proudly display the picture of this great American
[General Robert E. Lee] *on my office wall.*
　　　　　　—President Dwight D. Eisenhower, 1960

UNTIL THE ADVENT of the neo-Marxist cabal seeking to destroy every positive virtue of Western Christian Civilization, Robert
E. Lee and his Confederate associates were admired and respected.
But as events have demonstrated, respect for General Lee and the
common Confederate soldier is "gone with the wind." America's
radical leftists have and are maintaining a steady narrative of hate
against the men who wore the Gray in defense of their homeland
during the War for Southern Independence. As the iconic representative of all things Confederate and Southern, General Robert
E. Lee and his memorials have been targeted for "conceptualization"[1] and ultimate destruction by neo-Marxists. The hideous
false narrative promoted by neo-Marxists is based upon two false
concepts of the war. First, the idea that secession is tantamount to

---

1　Conceptualization is the act of forming a general notion of an idea. Radical leftists use
this term and concept to reinterpret and explain away ideas that they view as obstacles to the
advancement of the leftist agenda.

1

treason, and second, Lee and his fellow Confederates were fighting to defend and promote slavery. In the following pages, these two falsehoods will be examined and exposed as false narratives.

Before exploring the neo-Marxist charges against Lee (and therefore against all Confederates), let us explore how some notable world leaders felt about General Lee. Winston Churchill, who was engaged in no less than three wars, the Second Boer War (1899 to 1902), World War I (1914 to 1918), and World War II (1939 to 1945), noted that "Lee was the noblest American who had ever lived and one of the greatest commanders known to the annals of war."[2] As noted above, President Eisenhower kept a photo of General Lee in his presidential office. Eisenhower correctly acknowledged that General Lee was "one of the supremely gifted men produced by our Nation... [Lee was] selfless almost to a fault...noble as a leader and as a man, and unsullied."[3] Eisenhower goes on to state "I simply say this: a nation of men of Lee's caliber would be unconquerable in spirit and soul."[4] President Theodore Roosevelt proclaimed Lee to be, "the very greatest of all the great captains that the English-speaking peoples have brought forth"[5] and that Lee's example helped to establish, "the wonderful and mighty triumph of our national life, in which all his countrymen, north and south share."[6] President Franklin D. Roosevelt's admiration for Lee was demonstrated when he stated that Lee was "one of our greatest American Christians and one of our greatest American gentlemen."[7] President John F. Kennedy recognized Lee as a gallant leader who with his brave followers helped "to

---

2   Winston Churchill, as cited in, Jack Kerwick, *Townhall*, 'Robert E. Lee: An American Hero,' May 23, 2017, Robert E. Lee: An American Hero (townhall.com) pulled 5/21/2024.

3   Eisenhower, *Ibid.*

4   *Ibid.*

5   Theodore Roosevelt, *Ibid.*

6   *Ibid.*

7   Franklin D. Roosevelt, *Ibid.*

reunite America in purpose and courage."[8] President Gerald Ford proclaimed that Lee "stood as the symbol of valor and of duty. The course he chose after the war became a symbol to all those who had marched with him in the bitter years towards Appomattox."[9] President Ronald Reagan even pointed out Lee's attitude toward secession and slavery when he declared that "this southerner who criticized secession and called slavery a great moral wrong...would become himself an American legend."[10] The previous statements are only a few such examples of such statements by great men who praised and lauded this quintessential American hero. Today, lesser men than these dominate the media, academia, and other outlets of information with half-truths and downright misinformation about not only General Lee, but most of Southern history.

As sad as it is to see and hear leftist commentators sully the name of Lee and his fellow Confederates, the action of so-called conservative commentators joining the left in its attack is both shocking and disgusting. Conservative commentators such as Sean Hannity, Jesse Watters (see Addendum I 'Jesse Muddy Watters'), and others act as the left's "wing-man,"[11] defending leftists as they go on the attack against all things Confederate. For example, when neo-Marxists proclaimed that Lee was a traitor and defender of slavery and therefore his monuments in New Orleans, Richmond, Charlottesville, and other places had to be removed, how did "conservatives" such as Hannity react? Yes, conservative commentators proclaimed that monuments should not be removed. But did they question the "logic" of the neo-Marxists' charge of treason and defenders of slavery leveled against the South? Did conservative commentators point out that in 1860, many Americans, both in the North and the South,

---

8   John F. Kennedy, *Ibid.*

9   Gerald Ford, *Ibid.*

10   Ronald Reagan, *Ibid.*

11   In aerial combat, the "wing-man" does not attack the enemy, rather he protects the attacker from being attacked, thus ensuring the attacker's goal of destroying the target.

believed that secession was constitutional? Failing that, did these so-called conservatives invite representatives from the Sons of Confederate Veterans or other pro-South groups to repudiate the slanderous lies of the left? Has Hannity, Watters, or any conservative commentator ever offered a cogent counterargument to the leftist's charge that secession was treason? Have these so-called conservative commentators questioned the neo-Marxist slur that the South fought to defend slavery? Regrettably, the answer to these questions is NO! Such inaction by conservative commentators provided neo-Marxists all the protection that any good "wingman" would provide.

Modern conservatives are neo-conservatives, aka, neo-cons. A neo-con cannot defend Lee or any Confederate because to do so, they would have to offer the American people the opportunity to hear "the rest of the story" about secession and slavery. Especially when it comes to the history of slavery, the guilt of the North and the Republican Party is a deep dark secret that neo-cons do not want to discuss. Neo-cons may boast about being in favor of small government and obeying the Constitution, but being wedded to Lincoln's philosophy that the Federal government is sovereign (supreme in all matters) and not the States, they sound and act more like big government leftists than they act like or sound like Thomas Jefferson, Patrick Henry, and company. Why is it that even after the election of Ronald Reagan (1980) and Donald Trump (2016), the Federal government cannot be controlled? The answer is both simple and difficult for neo-cons to embrace. By transferring sovereignty in the United States from "we the people" of the sovereign state to the Federal government (Union) the most fundamental and effective "check and balance" upon the Federal government has been destroyed. *The destruction of _real_ States' Rights, thereby creating a massive unquestionable centralized federal government, is the most important and corrosive action of Lincoln and the Republican Party.* It is the threat of nullification and/or secession by "we the people" of a sovereign state that continuously reminded the Federal government to abide by the limitations of the Constitution. The invasion and conquest of the Confederate States of America by the United States resulted in the Federal government becoming the *sole judge* of the limits of its power—what tyrant could ask for more? To be the sole judge of one's power is the earmark of tyranny. The next time a conservative commentator complains about Washington's Deep State, remember, the Deep State is the out-growth of and result of the destruction of <u>real</u> States' Rights, but Mr. neo-con will never admit that fact.

A Federal government that cannot be controlled by "we the people" of a sovereign state raised its ugly head in 2003 when the Federal government ordered Alabama to remove all Ten Commandments monuments on the grounds of Alabama courthouses. In 2010, this same big government behemoth ordered Arizona to "cease and desist" enforcing Federal laws on immigration, the very same laws that the Federal government refused to enforce. During the so-called COVID crisis, the Federal government ordered the shutdown of businesses, churches, and forced Americans to be injected with medication of unproven validity and safety and closed many outdoor events. These and a plethora of other tyrannical acts are possible because the Federal government is the *sole judge* of its power. But what about States' Rights? Can't we depend upon the protection of the Tenth Amendment? The sad reality in post-Lincoln America is that there is no such thing as States' Rights, only States' *privileges*. States are allowed the *privilege* of doing only those things that the supreme (sovereign) Federal government approves. In a letter to a friend, Thomas Jefferson expressed his fear of a supreme, therefore, all-powerful Federal government. Jefferson wrote, "I see...the rapid strides with which the federal branch of our Government is advancing toward the usurpation of all the rights reserved to the States, and the consolidation in itself of all powers, foreign and domestic...leave no limits to their power."[12]

---

12   Thomas Jefferson, as cited in, William B. Parker and Jonas Viles, eds., *Letters and Addresses of Thomas Jefferson* (Buffalo, NY: National Jefferson Society, 1903), 287.

Men such as Robert E. Lee fought long and hard to prevent such a government from exercising its tyrannical power over the people of the Confederate States of America. The failure of the Confederacy to maintain its independence assured not only that the people of the South would now live under an all-powerful central government but ultimately, every American would have Big Brother's ever-present eyes upon them. In response to Lord Acton's question to Lee about what was to become of the United States now that real States' Rights was lost, Lee stated: "I fear for my country when all the rights which once belonged to the States are transferred to Washington. At that time America will become *aggressive abroad and despotic at home*"[13][emphasis added]. Liberals, neo-cons, and neo-Marxists will clothe themselves in a fig-leaf loin-cloth to hide the nakedness of their illegal transformation of a republic of sovereign states (1787 to 1861) into a massive all-powerful federal government—the actual government that rules Americans today. This same federal government, at its will, can trample upon the religious liberty of any citizen; forcibly inject its citizens with medication of questionable safety and reliability; force its hideous sexual values upon children; and demand "protection" for so-called transgender perverts as they choose to dress and undress in front of children and adults. All of this and more has become the norm because of the failure of Lee and his fellow Confederates' effort to maintain a portion (C.S.A.) of the original Constitutional Republic that America's Founding Fathers established as a viable institution. Is it any wonder that those in control of the massive "perks and privileges" being dispensed by America's Deep State are seeking to sully the name of Lee and the Confederate States of America?

---

13   Letter from Robert E. Lee to Lord Acton, December 15,1866, 'The Acton-Lee Correspondence,' LewRockwell.com accessed June 19, 2013, www.lewrockwell.com/orig3/acton-lee.html.

Chapter II

TREASON

Treason against the United States shall consist only in levying war against them, or in adhering to their enemies, giving them aid and comfort. No person shall be convicted of treason unless on the testimony of two witnesses to the same overt act, or on confession in open court.

—Article III, Section 3, U.S. Constitution

FOR ALMOST ONE HUNDRED YEARS after the defeat of the Armies of the Confederate States of America, the charge of treason against Confederates was seldom heard. Yet, since the early 1990s, that charge is loudly proclaimed by neo-Marxists and seldom, if ever, challenged or questioned by neo-conservatives. Usually, the removal of General Lee's monuments is preceded by assaulting Lee's character as being the leader of a rebellion and therefore guilty of treason.

There are two very important facts that must be examined to determine if one is guilty of treason, as defined by the U.S. Constitution. First and foremost, is the individual charged with treason a citizen of the United States? After the Japanese attack on Pearl Harbor and the following four years, no Japanese P.O.W. was ever charged with treason against the United States. Why? Although caught "levying war against them" (the United States), the

7

prisoners of war were not citizens of the United States. Obviously, a non-citizen cannot be charged with treason. The second point is that there must be at least two witnesses to the said act of treason.

First, let us consider the issue of citizenship for Lee and any Confederate. Two events happened in Lee's life before he joined the military force of the Confederate States, (1) Lee resigned his commission as an officer of the United States military and (2) his home state of Virginia passed an ordinance of secession and formally announced she was no longer a part of the United States. When Virginia recalled those rights which she had voluntarily delegated to the Federal government, via the act of secession, Lee's citizenship reverted to his home State, Virginia. But where is it written that Virginia can recall its delegated rights? Let the Founding Fathers speak! The very words of Virginia's U.S. Constitution Ratification Document (1788) clearly state: "In the name and on behalf of the people of Virginia, declare and make known, that the *powers granted* under the Constitution, being derived from the people of the United States, *may be resumed by them*, whensoever the same shall be perverted to their injury or oppression, and that every power not granted thereby remains with them and at their will"[14] [emphasis added]. It should be noted that according to Article VII of the U.S. Constitution, each State, acting for itself and unpressured by any other force, ratified the Constitution. The delegates for Virginia clearly stated, "We the said Delegates, in the name and in behalf of the people of Virginia...." Virginia's act of secession transferred citizenship solely to Virginia and when Virginia acceded to the new union, Confederate States of America, all the citizens of Virginia became citizens of the Confederate States of America. The issue of the Constitutionality of secession will be discussed later but for now, let us consider citizenship as understood in 1860.

---

14   U.S. Constitution.net, 'Virginia's Ratification' Virginia's Ratification – The U.S. Constitution Online – USConstitution.net – U.S. Constitution.net accessed 5-27-24.

Anyone who thinks that the concept of the right of recalling delegated rights, i.e., secession, is just a Southern idea, should read the ratifying documents of New York and Rhode Island as they acceded to the new Union under the Constitution. Just as Virginia had done, similar, if not stronger language is used by these Northern States to notify the new Union and the world of their right to withdraw anything they were delegating to the Federal government. Here are the very words of New York's official document ratifying the new Constitution: "That all power is originally vested in, and consequently derived from the people, and that Government is instituted by them for their common interests, protection, and security...That the powers of Government may be re-assumed by the people, whensoever it shall become necessary to their happiness; that every power, jurisdiction, and right, which is not by the said Constitution clearly delegated to the Congress of the United States, or the departments of the Government thereof, remains to the people of the several States, or to their respective State governments."[15]

As noted in Article VII of the Constitution, the citizens of each State, acting for that State and no other, were the ones to ratify the Constitution. Of special interest is the fact that it took only 9 out of 13 States to give life to the new union/government under the Constitution. The new union was not authorized to force the other 4 States back into the union that had existed before the 9 States had withdrawn.[16] This act proves that originally, to be a citizen of the United States one had to be a citizen of a State. After all, it was the citizens of the State who had the responsibility of ratifying or rejecting the proposed Constitution. Simply put, citizenship in the State existed *before* the existence of the Federal government

---

15   New York's Ratification as cited in, Alexander H. Stephens, *A Constitutional View of the Late War Between the States: Its Causes, Character, Conduct, and Results* (1867: Harrisonburg, VA: Sprinkle Publication: 1994), vol. I, 271.

16   Before the adoption of the U.S. Constitution, the thirteen original states were members of a union under the Articles of Confederation. The act of ratifying the Constitution meant that those states so ratifying the Constitution were seceding from the first union/government of the thirteen original states and forming a new government.

and therefore, these United States. State citizenship is antecedent to United States citizenship. At the time of the adoption of the Constitution, it was assumed that citizenship resided in the State and therefore the United States but nowhere does the Constitution identify that an individual is a citizen of either.

Prior to the War for Southern Independence, the subject of State and United States citizenship had been discussed and debated. The majority view, the view held by Democrats and many Whigs, was that United States citizenship was derived from one being a citizen of one of the Sovereign States. Those living in one of the territories of the United States were United States citizens due to having lived or sojourned in one of the States. Federalists, especially men such as John Marshall and Joseph Story, held the view that Americans were citizens of the United States first and their States second. The Federalist view was so unpopular that the political party wedded to that view, the Federalist Party, died an early death, killed by the States' Rights view of the Constitution. Needless to say, up until 1860, the majority of Americans held to the States' Rights view that United States citizenship was derived from one's home State. "One view was that national citizenship was dependent on state citizenship...those who were state citizens under state law, and only those people, were citizens of the United States."[17] As many have noted, there were at least two views on citizenship but no clear-cut Constitutional definition of citizenship. Therefore, embracing the Tenth Amendment, States' Rights advocates strongly held to the theory that an individual's citizenship depended upon their State citizenship.

A sad example of the view of State citizenship bequeathing United States citizenship was displayed in a letter from Francis Key Howard, the grandson of Francis Scott Key, author of the Star-Spangled Banner. Howard, the editor of a Maryland newspaper had written several articles questioning Lincoln's authority to

---

17   A.R. Amar and J.C. Harrison, *National Constitution Center*, 'The Citizenship Clause.' Interpretation: The Citizenship Clause | Constitution Center accessed, 5-24-24.

Francis Key Howard, grandson of Francis Scott Key, was illegally imprisoned by Lincoln for exercising his First Amendment right of freedom of speech and freedom of the press.

use military force against the Southern States. On September 13, 1861, Francis Key Howard had the dubious distinction of becoming a prisoner of state, i.e., a political prisoner, in Fort McHenry. It should be noted that Howard was imprisoned for the act of exercising his First Amendment right of freedom of the press and freedom of speech. He was arrested on orders of the Lincoln Administration and treated as a military combatant. Every aspect of his civil liberties as defined and protected by the Bill of Rights, were completely trampled upon. While illegally imprisoned (much like those imprisoned for the so-called January 6th "insurrection"), Howard wrote to a friend: "I am a citizen of the State of Maryland, and of course of the United States. I was carried from my house at midnight, by armed men, who professed to be acting under the orders of the [Lincoln's] Secretary of State but who refused to produce any warrant whatever in justification of their proceedings... Nearly three months have elapsed since I have been imprisoned, and no charge has been or even can be preferred against me, for I have violated no law."[18] Notice how the grandson of the author of the Star-Spangled Banner proclaims first that he is a "citizen of the State of Maryland [and then] of course of the United States." Once a State is no longer part of the United States, its citizens cannot legally be charged with treason. William Rawle, author of one of the first textbooks on the United States Constitution, noted that if a state withdrew from the compact of union, "allegiance would necessarily cease on the dissolution of the society to which it was due."[19]

The legality of secession will be discussed in some detail in the following chapters. As shall be pointed out, secession and the right of secession was a political question, just like citizenship, and had many notable backers in the early part of the history of the United States, including both Northern and Southern U.S. Presidents.

---

18   Francis Key Howard, *Fourteen Months in the American Bastiles* (Baltimore, MD: Kelly, Hedian and Piet, 1863), 67.

19   William Rawle, *A View of the Constitution of the United States of America,* 2nd ed., (1829: The Scuppernong Press: Wake Forest, NC: 2020), 252.

TREASON

Recurring back to the Constitution's definition of treason, it is clearly stated that it requires at least two witnesses of the act to bring the charge of treason against an individual. By 1865, there were over three hundred thousand Confederate soldiers, sailors, and government (State and Confederate) officials to level the charge of treason against. If one includes the millions of people who are "adhering to their enemies, giving them aid and comfort" to the Confederacy, the number of potential "traitors" would be in the millions. Of these multi-millions of Confederates, how many were ever charged with "treason?" At least thirty-seven men were indicted for treason, but those indictments were dropped. President Jefferson Davis was indicted for treason and incarcerated, but he was never brought to trial. Why? The South always believed that Davis and the other indicted individuals were innocent because they were citizens of the Confederate States of America. Until his death in 1889, President Davis's desire was to be placed on trial and thereby bring the Cause of the South before the court of world opinion. In the estimation of Federal prosecutors, the case against Davis was "too complex and politically charged to be worth pursuing."[20] Davis viewed the trial as an attempt to vindicate himself and the South. "Jefferson Davis was apparently eager to defend himself in court. He intended to argue that secession had been legal in the hopes of publicly (and legally) vindicating himself and the entire Confederate movement."[21] The Federal government understood the danger of allowing Americans and the world to hear the correct view of secession. As many had noted, if Davis or any Confederate was brought to trial, the Federal government could lose in court everything they had gained on the battlefield.

20   'The Trial of Jefferson Davis Canceled, February 15, 1869,' The Trial of Jefferson Davis Canceled – February 15, 1869 – Richmond National Battlefield Park (U.S. National Park Service) (nps.gov) accessed 5-25-24.

21   Ibid.

Thomas Jefferson, Virgina, and John Quincy Adams of Massachusetts, both agreed that secession was legal and preferable to holding the Union together by force. Lincoln and the Republican Party did not get that memo!

Chapter III

Is Secession Treason?

It depends on the state itself...whether it will continue a member of the Union. To deny this right would be inconsistent with the principle on which all our political systems are founded, which is, that the people have in all cases, a right to determine how they will be governed.

—William Rawle, Philadelphia, PA 1829

AS PREVIOUSLY STATED, the right of the people of a state to secede from the Union was never viewed as un-American or treasonous when the Constitution was adopted. William Rawle, a Northerner and a close friend of George Washington and Benjamin Franklin, wrote and published one of the first textbooks on the United States Constitution, titled, *A View of the Constitution of the United States*. The first edition of this book was published in 1825, and the second edition of this book was published in 1829. Chapter XI of the 2nd edition of Rawle's book is titled, 'Of Treason Against the United States.' Nowhere in this chapter is there any indication that the act of secession would be equivalent to treason. Chapter XXXII of the 2nd edition of Rawle's book is titled, 'Of the Permanence of the Union.' In this chapter, Rawle explains how and under what circumstances a state would secede from the Union. This textbook was given an extensive review by, *The North American Review,* a Boston, Massachusetts journal. The reviewers proclaimed Rawle's book to be "a safe and intelligent guide"[22] for understanding the Constitution. Notice that this review was done a mere 31 years before Southern secession began. Eight years before Lincoln called for troops to invade and subdue the Southern States, Rawle's book was recommended to his students by Francis Lieber,[23] a well-known German-American jurist, political philosopher, and educator. It should be noted that Lieber recommended books on the Constitution that advanced the idea of state sovereignty and therefore the right of secession as well as books that advanced the idea of Federal sovereignty and therefore Federal supremacy. This dichotomy of political views demonstrates that, at that time, there was no clear and accepted view about where sovereignty resided in these United States. Many modern historians will assert that "the war settled that question." According to that logic, it only takes a more powerful individual or group and the passage of time to convert an act of rape into making love—such views are not logical but rather illogical! As President Jefferson Davis once said, "A question settled by violence is a question that goes unsettled."

If sovereignty belongs to "we the people" of a State, then secession is as American as apple pie. If sovereignty resides in the Federal government, then secession by a state is treason. Therefore, the question "Is secession Constitutional or is the act of secession treason," ultimately comes down to the location of sovereignty within these United States. Sovereignty is defined as the power and authority of a state to order its society via laws and regulations. It includes the right to make and execute laws, impose taxes, and make war, and treaties. A sovereign state does all this *free from outside compulsion.* Those, like Lee, who hold to the Jeffersonian States' Rights view of the Constitution, believe that sovereignty belongs to "we the people" of each state of the Union. The contrary view is the Hamiltonian Federal supremacy view of the Constitution which is based upon the idea that all the people

22 *The North American Review* (1826: New York: AMS Press, Inc., 1965), XXII, 450.

23 Francis Lieber, *On Civil Liberty and Self-Government* (1853: Philadelphia: J. B. Lippincott and Co., 1859), 270.

of the United States as "one nation" are sovereign. Advocates of Federal supremacy often misquote Article VI, section 2, which states in part, "This Constitution, and the laws of the United States which shall be made in pursuance thereof...shall be the supreme law of the land." Big government advocates stress the phrase "supreme law of the land" as if it means that all the acts of the Federal government are supreme and unquestionable. The most important phrase in Article VI, section 2, is "pursuance thereof." If the acts or actions of the Federal government are outside of its delegated power or run counter to the Constitution, those acts and actions are null and void. Even High Federalist, Alexander Hamilton, said as much.[24] The Jeffersonian view (States' Rights) empowers "we the people" of the sovereign state making the people at the State level capable of determining how we shall be governed. States' Rights places "we the people" of each individual state as sovereign, whereas, the Hamiltonian (High Federalist) view makes the Federal government, as the agent of "we the people," sovereign.

Lincoln and the Republican Party advanced three false narratives as the foundation for denying the right of secession. Lincoln stated, "The Union is older than the Constitution and, in fact, created them as States. The Union, and not themselves separately, procured their independence and their liberty. [Therefore], no state...can lawfully get out of the Union... The Union threw off their old dependence [allegiance to Great Britain] for them and made them States *such as they are* [emphasis added].[25] In the same address, Lincoln, with the full support of the Republican Party, ridiculed the idea of state sovereignty, as if it had never been embraced by America's political system. In his message to Congress, Lincoln declared, "Much has been said about the 'sovereignty' of the states, but the word even is not in the National Constitution, nor, as is believed, in any of the State

---

24   See, Alexander Hamilton, in 'The Federalist No. 33.'

25   Abraham Lincoln, "July 4th Message to Congress," July 4th, 1861.

constitutions."[26] These three false narratives were embraced by Lincoln and the Republicans in Congress in defense of their war upon the South. These false narratives were: (1) The Union is older than the States; (2) the Union created the States, "such as they are;" and (3) since the word "sovereignty" does not exist in the Federal Constitution, no State can be sovereign. These three falsehoods will be examined, seriatim.

Lincoln alleged that the Union was older than the States and that the States were never sovereign. The only union that existed before July 4th, 1776, was the union between each separate American colony and Great Britain. There was absolutely no formal governing agent (union) among the thirteen colonies of what was to become the United States. When a border dispute erupted in armed violence between Maryland and Pennsylvania, Lincoln's mystical union was nowhere to be found. It was the British Union that acted to correct the problem. In 1763, Great Britain sent two Englishmen, Charles Mason, and Jeremiah Dixon, to its colonies to settle the dispute, whereupon we derived the Mason-Dixon line.

When conflict erupted between the colonies and Great Britain, it was the action of the citizens of each separate colony that expelled Royal authority from their colony. After expelling all Royal authority from their colony, the colony began to perform the duties of a "free and independent" state. Lincoln's mystical union was nowhere to be found during this difficult process. The people of each distinct colony, acting for their own benefit and without any help from an unseen force called the "union," established themselves as an independent society. When these independent states realized that acting in unison against a common foe would be beneficial, they organized the First (1774) and Second Continental Congress (1775-81). As in the case of all "congresses" of sovereign states, each state was allowed one vote regardless of size and/or population. The Continental Congress had no power of legislation or power to enforce its resolutions. The Continental Congress could

---

26   *Ibid.*

suggest anything but <u>conclude</u> nothing. The power of action was completely in the hands of the legislatures of each sovereign state. Also, each delegate sent by a state to the Continental Congress could only vote as <u>authorized by their state</u>. Once again, we see the action of independent states and not some mystical union. When the Declaration of Independence was presented to the Continental Congress, the delegates could not vote for or against independence until authorized by their State—again, no mystical union is seen acting upon this issue, only the action authorized by each individual sovereign state. Whether dealing with the Continental Congress, the formation of the first government, the Articles of Confederation, the writing of the Constitution, and adoption of the Constitution, it was all authorized by the independent action of each sovereign State, un-directed or un-aided by some unseen and mystical union. It is obvious that the Union is not older than the States, nor did the Union create the States.

Lincoln's sophomoric understanding of the founding of these United States is apparent and demonstrated by his denial of the idea of State sovereignty. The very first government of these United States existed under the Articles of Confederation (1781 to 1789). Article II of the Articles of Confederation clearly and unequivocally proclaims, "Each state retains its _sovereignty_, freedom, and independence, and every Power, Jurisdiction and right, which is not by this confederation expressly delegated to the United States, in Congress assembled" [emphasis added]. Lincoln and every Republican either had never read Article II of the Articles of Confederation or willfully and I dare say, "criminally," ignored this historic fact. Remember, the justification that Lincoln and the Republican Party used to invade and conquer the Southern States was the idea that no State of these United States was then or ever had been "sovereign." Over a million American military and civilians died, the bulk of which were Southern, and vast amounts of treasure were sacrificed on an altar of this falsehood, thanks to Lincoln and the Republican Party.

Lincoln's absurd assertion that since the word "sovereignty" does not exist in the Federal Constitution, no State could be sovereign. Since "Christ" does not exist in the Constitution, does that mean that there are no Christians in the United States? It appears that Mr. Lincoln and his fellow Republicans were grasping at straws attempting to hide the nakedness of their unconstitutional invasion of the Confederate States of America. If, as Lincoln declared, a State cannot be sovereign because that word does not exist in the FEDERAL Constitution, does that mean that the Federal government itself is not sovereign? Lincoln's "logic" is nonsensical.

Lincoln also proclaimed that the word "sovereign" does not exist in any State Constitution. Yet, we read in Louisiana's Constitution, that Louisiana was a "free and independent state." A "free and independent" state is a sovereign state. In the Constitution of the State of New Hampshire, it is proclaimed that "The people of this Commonwealth have the sole and exclusive right of governing themselves as a free, *sovereign*, and independent State" [emphasis added]. In her Constitution, Massachusetts announces that "the people of the commonwealth have the sole and exclusive right to governing themselves as a free, *sovereign*, and independent state" [emphasis added]. It appears that these states understood that they were sovereign states—something that Lincoln and his fellow Republicans did not understand or chose to ignore.

Nothing proves that the right of secession was fully embraced by Americans from every section, not just the South, than the Hartford, Connecticut secession convention. The War of 1812 was very unpopular in the New England States. The conflict between the United States and Great Britain caused great economic distress in New England. Responding to this situation, the legislature of Massachusetts called for a meeting of the New England States to discuss seceding from the United States. These delegates met on December 15th, 1814, and passed the following resolution: "Some new form of confederacy should be substituted among those States which shall intend to maintain a federal relation to each other...Whenever it shall appear that these causes are radical and permanent, a separation, by equitable arrangement, will be preferable to an alliance by constraint, among nominal friends, but real enemies, inflamed by mutual hatred and jealousy, and inviting by intestine divisions contempt, and aggression." The real threat of New England secession, along with General Jackson's victory in New Orleans, in January 1815, assured an end to the War of 1812 and New England secession. The statement issued by these New England delegates makes a firm and bold argument for the American right of secession. Of great significance is the statement these New Englanders made about not using force to hold "nominal friends, but real enemies" in a government they do not wish to be a part of—Lincoln had another idea!

Mr. Lincoln's assertion that the States were not and had never been "sovereign" would have been shocking news to the men of the Continental Army. After the adoption of the Declaration of Independence, the members of the Continental Army took the following oath: "I acknowledge the thirteen United States of America, namely [the names of the thirteen states were then recited] to be free, independent and *sovereign* States" [emphasis added]. This same acknowledgment is written in the Treaty of Paris in which the British Empire recognizes the United States as thirteen "free, independent, and sovereign" states. Here also, the thirteen states are each named and denoted by Great Britain to be sovereign states. St. George Tucker, one of America's Founding Fathers, a wounded veteran of the War for American Independence, and a noted jurist, clearly refutes Lincoln's absurd assertion about the States having never been sovereign: Tucker proclaims: "From the monument of the revolution they became severally independent and sovereign states...possess and bound by no ties but of their own creation." The very words of an individual who fought the good fight for American independence completely destroys Lincoln's false narrative. These are just a few such examples that prove Mr. Lincoln was incorrect whereas, Lee and the South were right!

Chapter IV

WHAT PRICE UNION

If the bond of union be the voluntary consent of the people, the government may be pronounced to be free; where constraint and fear constitute that bond, the government is no longer the government of the people, and consequently, they are enslaved.

—St. George Tucker, 1803

ST. GEORGE TUCKER'S remarks about voluntary consent being the very essence of a free government and a government bound together by compulsion being the very essence of slavery point out what it takes to make a free government perpetual. If the union is a union of mutual respect and goodwill, the free government, i.e., "union," will last. But remove consent and replace it with coercion, especially the coercion of bloody bayonets, and one is left with a government ruling over its slaves.

Much has been said about the Union being perpetual. There have been two unions in the history of these United States that have denoted themselves as perpetual: United Colonies of New England, and the Articles of Confederation. In the constitutions of both, they are proclaimed to be perpetual, yet, both did not last more than ten years. The one union that did not proclaim itself to be perpetual is the Union under the Constitution of these United States. Of special note is the union under the Articles of

Confederation because this "perpetual" union died when nine of thirteen states of that union withdrew (seceded) from that union to form the new union under the Constitution.

What makes a union, "perpetual?" A marriage is an example of a perpetual union. That union is made by committing oneself to several vows. If these vows are kept, the union is perpetual. But if one or both of the parties to the marriage union break their vows and do not seek reconciliation, the "perpetual" union is broken. A political union, like a marriage union, is perpetual if the parties to the agreement keep their vows.

In the 1826 book, *Commentaries on American Law,* New Yorker James Kent, informs the reader how the Union was to be maintained when he noted that it was to be: "on the concurrence and goodwill of the parts, the stability of the whole depends."[27] Notice how this well-respected jurist proclaims that the Union is to be preserved, not at the point of a bloody bayonet but by the "concurrence and goodwill of the parts." Indeed, men cannot be free if at the point of a bloody bayonet, they are forced to associate politically or socially with those they seek to avoid.

James Kent seems to be echoing the idea if not the actual words of James Madison. In the debates over the adoption of the Constitution, James Madison pointed out that no government could be perpetual because the "safety and happiness" of society trumps government. Madison noted that "the safety and happiness of society are the objects at which all political institution must be sacrificed."[28] Madison not only informs us that the Union is held together by pursuing the "safety and happiness of society," but he also notes that if any governmental institution gets in the way of said "safety and happiness," it is the governmental institution, i.e., Union, that must be sacrificed, not the people's safety

---

27 James Kent, *Commentaries on American Law* (1826: New York: Da Capo Press, 1971), I, 196-96.

28 James Madison, *Federalist Papers, No. 43.*

and happiness. Now consider the words of Patrick Henry as he was discussing the ratification of the Constitution: "The first thing I have at heart is American *liberty,* the second thing is American *union.*"[29] Here we see both a Federalist (Madison) and an Anti-Federalist (Henry) agreeing that in these United States, liberty always trumps government. Any government, i.e., union, that must be "sacrificed" to protect liberty is not an everlasting or perpetual government. Nor does that union have a higher call to maintaining its existence than does liberty.

One very important point to understand is the danger to liberty if one group of people attempt to force another group of people to accept a government against their will. To force a people to accept a government against their will is to negate one of the most fundamental concepts that these United States were founded upon, which is, the <u>consent</u> of the governed. As the Declaration of Independence points out, "Governments are instituted among Men, deriving their just powers from the consent of the governed." Any government that exists without the free and unfettered consent of the people is an unjust and illegitimate government. But what happens if one group of people attempts to force their will upon those seeking to be free of that domination? The ultimate result is the loss of freedom for both groups. As Edmund Burke noted when Great Britain used force to compel the continuation of a once friendly relationship between the American Colonies and the mother country, "you impair the object by your very endeavors to preserve it. The thing [you] fought for is not the thing recovered."[30] Burke goes on to inform Parliament that if they were successful in the coercion of the Colonies, the thing they were seeking to regain will be, "depreciated, sunk, wasted, and consumed in the contest."[31] Burke's warning to Parliament was

---

29 Patrick Henry, as cited in, William W. Henry, *Patrick Henry: Life, Correspondence and Speeches* (1891: Harrisonburg, VA: Sprinkle Publication, 1993), III, 449.

30 Edmund Burke, "Speech on Conciliation with the Colonies," as cited in *The Norton Anthology of English Literature,* Third Edition (New York: W.W. Norton and Co., 1974), I, 2352.

31 *Ibid.*

fully realized by Lincoln, and the Republican Party's use of bloody bayonets to force a government upon an unwilling people. This coercion destroyed America's original Constitutional Republic of Republics and replaced it with a tyrannical Federal empire. While vociferously proclaiming they were saving the Union, by 1865, the original Union that they professed to be saving had been "depreciated, sunk, wasted, and consumed in the contest."

The danger of destroying the fundamental principle upon which these United States were established is why President Buchanan refused to use violence to "save the Union." He, like Burke, understood that such action would destroy America's original Union of free people living in sovereign States and replace it with an all-powerful and ultimately, tyrannical, Federal empire. When pressed to use force against the seceding States, on December 3, 1860, President Buchanan responded, "Our Union rests upon public opinion, and can never be cemented by the blood of its citizens shed in civil war. If it cannot live in the affections of the people, it must one day perish. Congress may possess many means of preserving it by conciliation, but the sword was not placed in their hand to preserve it by force." What holds the Union together? As noted previously, James Kent of New York said, "on the concurrence and goodwill of the parts, the stability of the whole depends." Also recall the words of James Madison, "the safety and happiness of society are the objects at which all political institution must be sacrificed." Although neo-cons take great pleasure in criticizing and disparaging President Buchanan for not using force to "save the Union," Buchanan was following the advice of many notable Americans.

Neo-conservatives such as Hannity, Watters, Ingram, and others are quick to condemn President Buchanan as weak and lacking resolve to solve the secession crisis. But was Buchanan the only United States President to hold the view that the Constitution does *not authorize* the Federal government to use bloody bayonets to "save the Union?" When faced with the possibility of several New England States seeking secession in 1814, President Thomas

Jefferson wrote that they [New England] should "call a convention of their State, and to require them to declare themselves members of the Union...or not members, and *let them go*. Put this question solemnly to their people, and their answer cannot be doubtful."[32] Jefferson rejects the use of coercion or war to force people back into a union in which the people feel that they are being oppressed. If forced back into such a union Jefferson warns that, "near friends falling out, never reunite cordially."[33] But Jefferson was not the only President to hold views on secession in line with Buchanan's view. John Q. Adams, the sixth President of the United States and son of the second President of the United States, John Adams, had this to say about secession, "If the day should ever come... when the affections of the people of the states shall be alienated from each other; when fraternal spirit shall give away to cold in-difference...far better it be for the people of the disunited states, *to part in friendship from each other, than to be held together by constraint*"[34] [emphasis added]. As previously explained using the analogy of the marriage union, if the vows of union are being maintained the union is perpetual. But once the vows (marriage vows as it relates to marriage and the Constitution as it relates to the Union of States) are broken, the union has been destroyed. The union given to us by America's Founding Fathers was "depre-ciated, sunk, wasted, and consumed in the contest." What modern Americans are left with is but a mere shadow of the original Union.

Although Lincoln and the Republican Party insisted that the coercion of bloody bayonets to "save the Union" was legitimate, it must be pointed out that no other United States President ever suggested this was a correct course of action. As noted, Thomas Jefferson of Virginia and John Q. Adams of Massachusetts both rejected Lincoln's method. James Madison, the third President of

---

32   Thomas Jefferson, as cited in, William B. Parker and Jonas Viles, eds., *Letters and Addresses of Thomas Jefferson* (National Jefferson Society, Buffalo, NY: 1903), 231.

33   *Ibid.*

34   John Q. Adams, cited in Joshua Horne, "John Quincy Adams on Secession," Discerning History, 27 July 2013, tinyurl.com/yywbqmok accessed 7-4-2020.

the United States, plainly announced that it was the "safety and happiness" that was superior to the life of any government, and a prominent jurist from New York instructed Americans that the way the Union was to be maintained was by "mutual benefit and goodwill." Bloody bayonets are not instruments for promoting the "mutual benefit and goodwill" or the "safety and happiness of a society."

A question few seem willing to ask is, what was the cost of Lincoln's disastrous method of "saving" the Union? In human terms, it cost almost 800,000 military lives. In terms of daily loss of lives, that would be 550 deaths every day for four years (1861 to 1865). Now, if we include the civilian lost because of the war, 99% of which are Southern, that number would increase to almost one million Americans or 685 Americans per day for four years! The population of the United States in 1860 was 31.4 million. The military deaths for the U.S. and C.S. were around 2-3%[35]. In 2020, the United States population was just over 331 million people or approximately ten times larger than in 1860. Today, if the U.S. suffered a 3% death rate for four years, the death rate per day would be 6,850 per day for four years or a staggering death total of over eight million Americans.

The financial cost to the United States and the Confederate States was 5.2 billion dollars. The Federal government spent 3.2 billion and the Confederate government spent 2 billion dollars.[36] The Federal government spent 2.2 million dollars per day for four years to force its will upon a people who only desired to be free of Yankee domination. In today's currency that would equal $22,000,000.00 per day for four years. The cost of war to prevent

---

35   Depending on the source used, estimated military deaths range from 625,000 to 825,000. Note this does not include civilians who died of starvation, lack of medical care, housing, and lawlessness. Nor does this include thousands of former slaves who were grossly mistreated by the invader.

36   David K. Thompson, Cambridge Core, 'Financing the War' Financing the War (Chapter 9)– The Cambridge History of the American Civil War accessed 5-29-24.

Southern Independence cannot be fully understood without looking at the sad financial consequences of Yankee invasion, destruction, and exploitation suffered by the citizens of the South.

Currently, most Americans view the South as a relatively impoverished and backward society. But has the South always been the home of poverty, disease, and under-educated people? As to the issue of poverty, it may come as a shock to many people but before Yankee invasion and conquest, the South had one of the world's highest individual incomes. This high level of income began while the South was still part of the British Union. This was noted by researchers from the University of California and Harvard University: "During the Colonial Era Southerners had average income well above those of New England or the Middle Colonies. In fact, Southern colonial wealth and riches do not surprise those who have researched this subject, but it may surprise some that even average free labor earnings were higher in the South."[37] What began during the colonial era, continued through the antebellum era in the South. In 1974, Nobel Prize-winning authors Robert W. Fogel, PhD, and Stanley L. Engerman, PhD, published an economic study on slavery. Fogel and Stanley's findings were published in *Time on the Cross: The Economics of American Slavery*. Fogel and Engerman's research destroyed the theory of an impoverished Antebellum South. They noted that the per capita income in the Antebellum South was vigorously growing faster than any other section of the nation. In other words, the South was not a region of poor ignorant whites. In a ranking of the nineteen most industrial nations in 1860, the South would rank number three, ahead of every European nation except Great Britain.[38]

---

37   Lindert and Williamson, as cited in, Kennedy and Kennedy, *Punished with Poverty* (Columbia, SC, Shotwell Publishing, SC: 2020), 15.

38   Fogel and Engerman, *Time on the Cross* (Boston—Toronto, Little, Brown, and Company: 1974), 256.

As sad as the economic results of Lincoln and the Republican Party taking the low road to emancipation, Reconstruction, both active Reconstruction and passive Reconstruction live with America to this day. The sad result of Reconstruction is fully explained by Ron Kennedy in *Reconstruction: Destroying the Republic-Creating an Empire*. The consequence of Radical Republican Reconstruction is evident today in Modern Day Reconstruction that began circa 1965.

Republican-sponsored Reconstruction Amendments and enforcement legislation paved the way for an unlimited expansion of Federal authority over "We the people" at the local, state, and national level. This expansion included the right of the Federal Government to prohibit Southerners in the military from displaying symbols of their Southern heritage. In a 1990 case, the Supreme Court upheld the "right" of a federal judge to order the Kansas City, Missouri, school board to raise taxes to pay for a wide-ranging magnet school plan designed to achieve racial integration. During the China COVID scare, the Federal Government engaged in flagrant violations of the Constitutional rights of freedom of assembly, freedom of speech, and freedom of religion. Yet, America's political slaves (with few exceptions) accepted Federal authority and meekly obeyed. During Active Reconstruction (1866-77) and Passive Reconstruction (1877-1965), America's Republic of Sovereign States was dissolved, and the once Sovereign States were unconstitutionally merged into "one nation indivisible." During Active Reconstruction, the Republican Party engineered this radical and unconstitutional perversion of America's original government—a Constitutionally limited Republic of Sovereign States. During Passive Reconstruction (1877-1965), both national political parties endorsed this unconstitutional, therefore illegitimate, change and used their political and social power to enforce these changes. The reason is simple: the traditionally conservative South became the timid and pacified South, offering no real resistance to this radical, illegal, and unconstitutional perversion of America's legitimate Federal Government. Politicians in both national political parties began to enjoy the perks, privileges, and power available to those working with the political *status quo*. The decentralized, Constitutionally limited, Republic of Sovereign States morphed into the tyrannical system of a centralized, indivisible, supreme Federal Government controlled by Northern and eventually Globalist ruling elites.

The next to last stage of any society, leading directly to its final stage of collapse, is "its forcible political unification in a centralized state."[39]

A NEW TYPE OF RECONSTRUCTION IN THE MODERN ERA—POST-1965.

The unstoppable growth of governmental intrusion into the private life of "We the people" after the passage of President Lyndon Baines Johnson's Great Society programs (1964-1968) has been noted by modern-era political observers. One wrote that the "growth of imperial power of the White House," is today beyond the control of the people.[40] He noted that America had become an "overextended empire."[41] He pointed out that it makes no difference who is in the White House or which party controls Congress, the established "mode of thought" in the political *status quo* is one of endless war and the continuous "application of military force."[42] This is something that President Eisenhower warned Americans about in his final address to the American people as President. He warned of the existence of something more powerful than "We the people" called the military-industrial complex. The coalition of big

---

39 Arnold Toynbee, as cited in, *Rethinking the American Union for the Twenty-First Century* Dr. Donald Livingston editor (Pelican Publishing Co., Gretna, LA: 2013), 172.

40 Tom Englehardt, *Shadow Government: Surveillance, Secret Wars, and a Global Security State in a Single-Superpower World* (Haymarket Books, Chicago, Ill.: 2014), 25.

41 *Ibid*, 118.

42 *Ibid*.

business, big financial institutions, and big government plus the ever-increasing welfare state have created an American government that is more national socialist than free market capitalism.[43]

The government now tracks private citizens directly or indirectly through its connections with monopolistic tech giants. The Central Intelligence Agency (CIA), as originally organized, was prohibited from becoming involved in domestic politics. But recently it went around that prohibition by having its contacts in "friendly" foreign agencies investigate Americans and then hand the results over to the CIA.[44] This is but one example of the invisible tentacles of the Deep State that control America regardless of which political party is supposedly in control of "our" government—indeed the political parties are a major supporter of the Deep State's *political status* quo.

The weaponization of the FBI in the 2016 Presidential campaign is another example of the Reconstruction era type of corruption that exists today in "our" Federal Government. FBI agent Linda Page expressed her concern about the possibility of Trump becoming president in an e-mail to her lover and fellow FBI agent Peter Strzok. Strzok was Chief of Counterespionage Section of the FBI. Page texted her fellow FBI agent Peter Strzok, "[Trump] is not going to become president, right?" Strzok replied "No. No, he won't. We'll stop it."[45] Here you see the depth to which our once-vaunted free government has sunken. The bureaucrats hold more power than "We the people!" The ruling elite have no respect for "We the people" in what they refer to as "fly-over country." They view "We the people" as being "irredeemables, deplorables, bitter clingers, and smelly Walmart shoppers." The radical change

---

43   John, Lukacs, *Democracy and Populism: Fear and Hatred* (Yale University Press: 2005), 41, 139-40.

44   Andrew C. McCarthy, *Ball of Collusion: The Plot to Rig an Election and Destroy a Presidency* (Encounter Books, NY: 2019), 24.

45   Strzok and Page as cited in, *Ibid*, 195.

in America's original Federal Government produced by Active Reconstruction made Modern Day Reconstruction not only possible but unavoidable.[46]

---

46   See, Kennedy, James Ronald, *Reconstruction: Destroying the Republic-Creating an Empire* (Shotwell Publishing, Columbia, SC: 2024).

Lysander Spooner, Massachusetts abolitionist and civil libertarian, declared that the North did not fight the war to free slaves but to dominate the South. Spooner correctly stated that rather than freeing slaves, all Americans were now slaves to an all-powerful Federal government.

Chapter V

DID CONFEDERATES FIGHT TO DEFEND AND PROMOTE SLAVERY?

In this enlightened age, there are few I believe, but will acknowledge, that slavery as an institution, is a moral and political evil in any country.

— Robert E. Lee

Only with the evolution of modern historical thought, heavily influenced by the ideas and tactics of Marx and Stalin, did the Civil War become "all about slavery."

— Dr. Samuel Mitcham, Jr.

Slavery is no more the cause of this war than gold is the cause of robbery.

—Governor Joel Parker, New Jersey, 1863-66

THE FOLLOWING CHAPTER is a summary of the evidence that the South did not fight the War for Southern Independence to protect slavery. A thorough examination of this topic was done in 2020 by retired historian, Dr. Samuel Mitcham, in his book *It Wasn't About Slavery*. This work, along with many other such books, is recommended to the reader for a complete understanding of slavery and the War.

The misuse of the issue of slavery in American history was summarized by President Jefferson Davis: "No subject [slavery] has been more generally misunderstood or more persistently misrepresented."[47] This "misrepresentation" about Southern slavery has led both liberal and conservative commentators to promote the myth that Southern soldiers were fighting to secure the right to own slaves. The simple fact that from 70% to 80% of the Confederate military consisted of men who were not slave-holders, should cause a reasonable person to stop and reconsider the myth that the South was fighting to protect slavery. In addition to that fact is the fact that the only state to be admitted to the Union while Lincoln was president, and the Republican Party-controlled Congress was the slave state of West Virginia. Robert E. Lee's statement, "that slavery as an institution, is a moral and political evil in any country"[48] is an example of how far the South had come in its effort to emancipate its slaves. The people of no other nation have ever, at their personal expense, freed more enslaved people than the South.

Many Confederate Veterans were eager to formally declare that they were not fighting to protect slavery. One such account is given by Robert Stiles, a Virginian and a graduate of Yale University. When war became inevitable, he volunteered to serve in the Richmond Howitzers as a private and rose to the rank of major by the end of the war. To the charge that he and his fellow volunteers were fighting for slavery, Stiles noted, "Surely, it was not for slavery they fought. The great majority of them had never owned a slave and had little or no interest in that institution. My own father, for example, had freed his slaves long years before... The great conflict will never be properly comprehended by the man who looks upon

---

47   Jefferson Davis, *The Rise and Fall of the Confederate Government* (William Coats Publisher, Nashville, TN: 1881), vol. I, p. 3.

48   Robert E. Lee, as cited in, Douglas S. Freeman, *R. E. Lee* (Charles Scribner's Sons, NY: 1947), vol. I, p. 372.

it as a war for the preservation of slavery."[49] This young man, the son of a Southern emancipationist, destroys the neo-Marxist false narrative about the South fighting to promote slavery. Note that Major Stiles, C.S.A., points out that most Confederates did not own slaves, and his family, like so many other Southerners, were advocates of ending slavery.

Even the Governor of New Jersey, Joel Parker, stated that slavery did not cause the war any more than "gold is the cause of robbery."[50] Cars do not cause car-jacking and likewise, slavery did not cause the War. This concept was echoed by George Lunt, a Massachusetts lawyer, editor, historian, and author of *Origin of the Late War* (1866). In his book, Lunt notes that "slavery caused the War like property causes theft."[51] Even a Massachusetts abolitionist, Lysander Spooner, pointed out that the North fought the war not to free slaves but to secure control of Southern markets[52] and secure control of the Federal government.[53] Spooner boldly states that by using force to compel the Southern States back into the Union, the North introduced political slavery throughout the Union: "On the part of the North, the war was carried on, not to liberate slaves...the number of slaves, instead of having been diminished by the war, has been greatly increased...there is no difference in principle—only in degree—between political and chattel slavery."[54]

---

49   Robert Stiles, as cited in, Samuel W. Mitcham, Jr., *It Wasn't About Slavery* (Regnery History, Washington, DC: 2020)157.

50   Parker, *Ibid*, 155.

51   George Lunt as cited in, Walter D. Kennedy, *The Confederate Myth-Buster* (The Scuppernong Press, Wake Forest, NC: 2019), 196.

52   Lysander Spooner, *No Treason: The Constitution of No Authority* (1870: Free Patriot Press, http://Freepatriot-Press.com 76-7. Accessed 2009.

53   *Ibid*.

54   *Ibid*.

Neo-Marxists depend heavily on what is known as a "univariate" analysis to "prove" that the South fought the war to promote slavery. A univariate analysis only looks at one symptom of a problem to the exclusion of other relevant facts. One of their favorite methods is to quote any Southern statesman or document that mentions slavery as a "positive good." Citing the Mississippi Ordinance of Secession is one example of such a tactic used by neo-Marxists. What these people do not mention is the fact that the Mississippi legislature and governor had already condemned slavery and were seeking a solution to the issue as early as 1820. With the advent of the Yankee radical abolition movement, with their efforts to foment or provoke slave revolts, the Southern effort of taking the high road to emancipation was destroyed. Those who are quick to condemn the South will overlook the fact that the same concept about slavery was held by Northerners. "Those people" do not like to be reminded that slavery existed in Massachusetts for 74 years longer than it existed in Mississippi.[55]

Here is an example of the use of a univariate analysis. During the Lincoln-Douglas Debates, Abraham Lincoln pronounced himself as a white supremacist. Lincoln plainly stated, "I will say, then, that I am not, nor ever have been, in favor of bringing about in any way the social and political equality of the white and black races...that there is a physical difference between the white and black races...I am in favor of having the superior position assigned to the white race."[56] Using just one factor in Lincoln's political life, we can conclude that he and the Republican Party were white supremacist radicals.

---

55   Massachusetts began its commerce in slaves in 1640, Massachusetts legalized slavery in 1641. Massachusetts began a system of gradual emancipation of slaves in 1780, therefore, slavery existed in Massachusetts for 139 years. The Mississippi Territory became part of the U.S. in 1800, slavery ended in Mississippi in 1865 or 65 years.

56   Abraham Lincoln, 'Lincoln Douglas Debate' September 1858, as cited in, Kennedy and Kennedy, *The South Was Right!* (Shotwell Publishing, Columbia, TN: 2020), 3rd ed., pp. 36-37.

Like most wars, the War for Southern Independence revolved around money more than anything else. Surely, slavery was an issue but not THE issue in the war. From the beginning of the Union issues like Northerners selling the use of the Mississippi River to Spain thereby pushing Southern commerce into Northern ports, the use of tariffs to force Southerners to purchase Northern goods rather than foreign goods, attempting to keep Southerners out of the commonly held territories, and the misappropriate spending tax revenue for Northern projects, are just a few of the many differences between the North and the South. Add to this the effort of Radical Abolitionists to incite a slave revolt that would threaten not just slave-holders but all Southerners, and the time was ripe for separation. From London, England, Charles Dickens noted the real cause of the War when he wrote: "The Northern onslaught upon slavery was no more than a piece of specious humbug designed to conceal its desire for economic control of the Southern states."[57] As one can see, it was not just one item that caused this war. For a more detailed account of how other issues were involved in pushing the South to secede from Northern domination, see Chapter 2, 'The Yankee Empire's Myth of History' in *The South Was Right!*[58]

In 1835, a resident of Maine, Joseph H. Ingraham, toured the South taking note of the vast differences between the North and the South. He was especially interested in how slaves were treated by Southerners. After a long visit, he published *The South-West By A Yankee*. Ingraham was impressed with how well slaves in the South were treated and how much social interaction took place between the races. Ingraham noted that indeed slavery needed to end but he also recognized that it had to be done to benefit both the former slave-holder and the slave. Ingraham noted, "When the chains of the slave are broken in pieces, it must be by a southern hand—and thousands of southern gentlemen are already extending

---

57   Charles Dickens, as cited in, Mitcham, p. 111.

58   Kennedy and Kennedy, *The South Was Right!* (Shotwell Publishing, Columbia, SC: 2020), 3rd ed., pp.. 21-78.

their arms, ready to strike the blow."[59] What Ingraham is explaining is what Jefferson Davis called the "high road to emancipation." Unfortunately for all Americans, Lincoln and the Republican Party rejected the high road and took the low road of emancipation. As Lee noted, slavery needed to end but it had to be done by those who were motivated by love for their fellow humans and not radicals using people to advance a revolutionary agenda.[60]

---

59   Joseph H. Ingraham, *The South-West By A Yankee* (Harper & Brothers, NY: 1835), Vol. I, Forward. 1

60   Lee, as cited by Freeman, Vol. I, p. 372.

Conclusion

Lee Was NOT a Traitor

REGARDLESS OF HOW AMERICANS FEEL today, until the election of Lincoln, no United States President boldly announced that the Union had a right to force a State to agree with a presidential view. As often stated, the victor writes and enforces HIS view of a conflict. Today, Americans, both in the North as well as in the South, are inundated with the victor's views about secession, treason, and slavery. Nevertheless, as has been demonstrated herein, notable Americans, including no less than four former United States Presidents, including Thomas Jefferson, view secession as an option for the people of any State of these United States. On the other hand, no former U.S. President ever stated that the Federal government had the right to invade, murder, pillage, and at the point of a bloody bayonet, force a once free people into a government they did not desire to be a part. When Lincoln and the Republican Party invaded the Southern States, there were five former U.S. Presidents alive. Not one of the five endorsed Lincoln's war. One former president boldly stated that it was unconstitutional for the Federal government to use military force to coerce a State; one clearly stated he would do nothing to assist Lincoln's evil effort; one became an elected member of the Congress of the Confederate States of America; and the other two never joined the Republican Party and were not enthusiastic about Lincoln's war.

In his first inaugural address, Ronald Reagan clearly stated that the Federal government did not create the states but the states created the Federal government. Reagan also declared that the Federal government was a limited government and could not act beyond what was authorized in the Constitution. Lincoln and the Republican Party (1861) said that the Union created the states "such as they are." Lincoln was the real traitor to the real American Union.

The sad fact is that Lincoln's war did not save the Union given to us by America's Founding Fathers, rather, Lincoln and the Republican Party's war upon the South destroyed that Union and gave America a government that is now the *sole judge* of its power. Such power is the nursery of all the world's tyrannical governments. The charges of "treason" and "defending slavery" are nothing less than a smoke-screen to hide the Republican Party's guilt in destroying America's original Constitutional Republic of sovereign States and establishing Deep State Big Government.

The most damaging result of the Federal government's victory over the Confederate States of America is the destruction of REAL States' Rights. Where once the sovereign State stood between its citizens and an aggressive and abusive Federal government, with the death of REAL States' Rights, the Federal government now is supreme in *all* areas of life for every American. As Lysander Spooner of Massachusetts noted in 1870, when government becomes more powerful than the citizens, all Americans now exist in a state of political slavery. As he noted, rather than ending slavery, the North increased the number of slaves in America.

How can the deleterious result of the death of REAL States' Rights be corrected? How can Lincoln's political slaves in America once again live in a free nation where government exists by the "consent of the governed?" How can Americans once again live in a nation that honors the principle of Patrick Henry who declared: "The first thing I have at heart is American *liberty,* the second thing is American *union.*" When this concept is once again the basis of the American government, liberty will always trump government. If the people of the United States unite and demand a return to REAL States' Rights, we will be a free people. Until the "powers that be" in Washington, New York, and other centers of money and power, are put on notice that "we the people" of the sovereign States have the ultimate right to judge for ourselves how we are governed, we will continue to be serfs at best and slaves at worst to the powers-that-be in the Deep State. Nothing less than a return to REAL States' Rights, inclusive of the rights of Nullification and

Secession, will solve the ongoing problem of out-of-control Big Government. The following text is of a proposed amendment to the Constitution that will begin the process of making the Federal government our servant instead of our master.

The Sovereign State Constitutional Amendment

These United States of America are a Republic of Sovereign States. The Federal Government derives its authority from the consent of the governed residing within their respective Sovereign State. Each Sovereign State is the agent of the people thereof. The Federal Government formed by the compact of the United States Constitution is the agent of the Sovereign States. Federal authority shall be supreme in all areas specifically delegated to it by the Constitution. All acts or legislation enacted pursuant to the Constitution shall be the supreme law of the land. Each Sovereign State, as with all Sovereigns, reserves the right to judge for itself as to the constitutionality of any act of its agent, the Federal Government.

Section I. Each Sovereign State specifically reserves the right to interpose its sovereign authority between acts of the Federal Government and the liberties, property, and interests of the citizens of the state, thereby nullifying federal acts judged by the state to be an unwarranted infringement upon the reserved rights of the state and the people thereof.

1. State nullification of a federal act must be approved by a convention of the state.

2. Upon passage of an act of nullification, all federal authority for the enumerated and nullified act(s) shall be suspended within the nullifying state.

3. Upon formal acceptance of nullification by three-fourths of the conventions of the states, including the original nullifying state, the enumerated federal act(s) shall be prohibited in the United States of America and its territories.

4. Upon formal rejection of nullification by three-fourths of the conventions of the states, the enumerated federal act(s) shall be presumed to be constitutional, notwithstanding any judgment of any federal or state court.

5. Until or unless there is a formal approval or rejection by the conventions of the states, the nullified federal act(s) shall remain non-operative as to the original and any additional nullifying states. A state that in its convention ratifies a particular act of nullification shall be construed to have nullified the same act as enumerated in the initiating state's nullification.

6. No federal elected official, agent, or any individual working within or associated with any branch of the federal government may harass or attempt to harass, intimidate, or threaten a Sovereign State or the people thereof for exercising their rights under this amendment. No federal elected official, agent, or any individual working within or associated with any branch of the federal government shall attempt to influence or use their office to attempt to influence the deliberations of the people regarding the nullification of a federal act(s) or the acceptance or rejection of a nullified federal act(s).

7. Any United States military officer, noncommissioned officer or federal official or agent who carries out or attempts to carry out any order by a federal official, officer, or agent to deny or hinder the

people of a Sovereign State from exercising their rights under this amendment shall be subject to the offended state's laws and may be tried accordingly. Jurisdiction in such cases is specifically denied to all federal courts, military courts, or any other court other than the courts of the offended state.

Section II. The government and people of these United States approve the principle that any people have a right to abolish the existing government and form a new one that suits them better. This principle illustrates the American idea that government rests on the consent of the governed and that it is the right of a people to alter or abolish it at will whenever it becomes destructive of the ends for which it was established. Therefore, the right of a Sovereign State to secede peacefully from the union voluntarily created by the compact of the Constitution is hereby specifically reserved to each state.

1. An act of secession shall be executed by a convention of the people of the state.

2. The seceded state shall appoint representatives to negotiate settlement of all debts owed the Federal Government, the purchase of federal properties within the Sovereign state, and the removal of federal military installations and personnel.

3. Upon acceptable arrangement for the payment of sums owed the Federal Government, the representatives may negotiate treaties of friendship, common defense, and commercial relations. Said treaties are subject to the same constitutional ratification as other treaties.

4. Readmission of a seceded state shall follow the same constitutional requirements as for any new state.

5. No federal elected official, agent, or any individual working within or associated with any branch of the federal government shall attempt to influence the people of the Sovereign State regarding their decision to secede from, remain with, or join this union.

6. Any United States military officer, noncommissioned officer, or federal official or agent who carries out or attempts to carry out any order by a federal official, officer, or agent to deny or hinder the people of a Sovereign State from exercising their rights under this amendment shall be subject to the offended state's laws and may be tried accordingly. Jurisdiction in such cases is specifically denied to all federal courts, military courts, or any other court other than the courts of the offended state.

The duty of the people of the Sovereign State to exercise their inalienable right to govern themselves is a right that existed before the formation of the Federal Government, and therefore, nothing in this amendment shall be interpreted in such a manner as to deem the Federal Government to be the donor of the rights as exercised by the people of the states.

Addendum I

Jesse "Muddy" Watters
More Anti-South Bigotry[61]

ONE OF THE FEW FOX NEWS PROGRAMS I faithfully watch is 'Jesse Watters Primetime.' Watters, with his signature sign-off refrain "I am Watters, and this is my world," has become a well-known neo-conservative, i.e., neo-con, Fox commentator. I enjoy his style and agree with 90% of Mr. Watters' commentary. Unfortunately, there are times when Watters says something that makes me want to throw my shoe, or better yet, a .45 APC round at my TV. Such an incident arose shortly after Colorado's woke Supreme Court upheld the removal of President Trump from Colorado ballots. Like most reasonable people, Mr. Watters understood that this action was highly political and un-Constitutional. So, what is my problem?

Like a faithful neo-con, Mr. Watters felt it necessary to slander all Southerners by linking the Confederacy with Colorado's hideous woke action. Mr. Watters and virtually every neo-con "talking head" parroted a repugnant lie about the Southern States in 1860. Mr. Watters, holding a B.A. in history from Trinity College in Hartford, Connecticut, should not have fallen for such a verifiable misstatement. One is left feeling that someone who was educated

---

61   This article was originally published in the March/April 2024 issue of the *Confederate Veteran* magazine (Columbia, TN: Sons of Confederate Veterans).

49

at a prestigious Connecticut college and yet actively promotes such bigoted anti-South propaganda must be acting from an anti-South animus and not from a lack of education.

According to Watters and other neo-cons, "Colorado kicking Trump off the ballot is just like ten Southern States in 1860, kicking Lincoln off their state ballot." Watters, a Yankee-educated neo-con, is promoting a Marxist-style half-truth in the pursuit of winning points at any cost. True, Lincoln was not on the ballot in ten Southern States. Yet, our well-educated and powerful neo-con talking head overlooked one succinct fact; Lincoln was NEVER on those state ballots. You cannot "kick" someone off a ballot who was never on that ballot! At this point, we need to educate our neo-con nemesis. These ten states plus three other sovereign states subsequently exercised the American Right of self-government by recalling their delegated Rights from the Federal government and forming a new government by the "consent of the governed."

One of the most important factors that led to the secession of the Southern States was the fact that Mr. Lincoln was elected by a purely *sectional* political party. Up until Lincoln's election, national political parties were organized in every state and the ticket for the president of the United States was a "balanced" ticket. A "balanced ticket" had both the North and the South represented on the party's ballot. If a presidential candidate was from the North, the vice-presidential candidate was from the South and vice versa. A balanced ticket helped to preserve the "mutual benefit and goodwill" of each part of the Union. In his 1796 Farewell Address, Washington warned the nation about the evils of politics by sectionalism, that is, rule of the whole Union by one or two sections of the Union (North versus South, East versus West, or such combinations). Washington noted that if one section or as he put it, "district," controls too much power it could use that power to, "misrepresent the opinions and aims of other districts." As he noted, such action by one sectional party would create "jealousies and heart burnings which spring from these representations: *they tend to render alien to each other those who ought to* *be bound together by **fraternal affection**"* [emphasis added]. As Washington noted, sectionalism would destroy the Union of "fraternal affection" and should be greatly feared.

In 1860, there were four political parties contending for the office of president: Constitutional Union (former Whig, disgruntled Democrats, and others), Northern Democrat, Southern Democrat, and Republican. Three of the above parties had a "balanced" ticket, the Republican Party did not. The Constitutional Union Party nominated Sen. John Bell of Tennessee for president and Edward Everett of Massachusetts for vice president; Northern Democrats nominated Sen. Stephen Douglas of Illinois for president and Sen. Herschel V. Johnson of Georgia for vice president; Southern Democrats nominated John C. Breckinridge, former United States Vice President, for president and Sen. Joseph Lane of Oregon for vice president; Republican Party nominated Lincoln of Illinois for president and Sen. Hannibal Hamlin of Maine for vice president. Mr. Watters, it appears that the South had been "kicked off" the GOP ballot!

In 1860, the Republican Party did not have one elected official in the ten states Watters so flippantly slandered. There were three Southern States where Lincoln was on the ballot, Virginia, Kentucky, and Missouri. In Virginia, Lincoln received 1.13% of the popular vote, in Kentucky, he received less than 1% of the vote, and in Missouri' he received 10% of the vote. Receiving only 39% of the national vote, having no elected Republicans holding office in these ten Southern States and no organized Republican Party in these states, how can it be maintained that "Lincoln was kicked off the ballot in the South?" With no elected Republicans in ten Southern States and receiving a pitifully small vote in three other Southern States where he was on the ballot, is it any wonder that in response to his election by a purely sectional party, the Southern States struck for independence?

When dealing with Southern history and heritage, both neo-cons and neo-Marxists follow the "party-line" of an evil slave-holding and treasonous South seeking to promote slavery and destroy the Union. This false narrative is never allowed to be challenged by the defenders of the real Union. The real Union was the Union given to us by America's Founding Fathers. That Union was held together by "fraternal affection," "mutual benefit and goodwill," and to preserve the "safety and happiness" of the parts of the whole. Neo-cons and neo-Marxists will do all in their power to prevent this message from reaching Americans.

How many times has Fox News asked a spokesman from the Sons of Confederate Veterans to answer the spurious charges leveled against the South of being "defenders of slavery" or "traitors to the United States?" Fox has plenty of time to interview Lincoln sycophant Victor David Hanson but not a representative from the Sons of Confederate Veterans. Fox News, not unlike its associate news outlet, MSN, simply regurgitates the same ideas as announced and promoted by Karl Marx and Friedrich Engels. It was Marx and Engels who served as Lincoln's virtual European propaganda ministers during the War. Addressing the International Workingmen's Association in 1864, Karl Marx praised Lincoln and his efforts for the "reconstruction of a social world." Marx, like neo-cons and neo-Marxists, viewed the War for Southern Independence as a war to protect and promote slavery. Marx also praised Lincoln for his efforts of promoting the idea that the United States should be "one great democratic republic." In an article published in 1848 for the advancement of the Communist Party in Germany, Marx and Engels noted the very *first* thing needed to promote communism was to change the Federal Republic of Germany, a republic composed of many sovereign states, into "one nation indivisible." In a letter to fellow communist and Union General, Joesph Weydemeyer, Engels noted what the defeat of the Confederate States would mean for promoting communism: "The preliminaries of the proletarian [communist] revolution, the measures that prepare the battleground and clear the way for us, such as a single and indivisible republic...are now *convenu* [taken for granted]." In another letter to Weydemeyer, Engels stated his belief that the defeat of the Confederacy would "doubtless determine the future of America for hundreds of years to come." These previous statements by Marx and Engels should make it clear to those surrounded by the "muddy Watters" of liberalism, why Confederate monuments must be destroyed, Confederate heroes slandered, and why the truth about the War for Southern Independence, Lincoln, and the GOP cannot be allowed a fair hearing.

Watters and other neo-cons are rightfully outraged at the thought of the Federal government being "weaponized" against political opponents. But where did this act of "weaponizing" the Federal government against one's political opponents begin? Mr. Watters, it was the Republican Party that had an opposition politician, a Northern Democrat, arrested, tried, and convicted by a *military* court. Representative Clement C. Vallandigham of Ohio is the only elected official in American history to be tried, convicted, and banished from the United States. The arrest, trial, and banishment of Rep. Vallandigham was done with the approval of Lincoln and the Republican Party. Lincoln's Administration shut down newspapers that opposed his war, he had private mail opened and inspected, and ministers of the Gospel in the North and South were arrested if they were suspected of "disloyalty" by not praying for Lincoln. One of the newspaper editors arrested by Lincoln, tried and imprisoned by the military, not civil authorities, or civil courts, was Francis Scott Howard, the grandson of Francis Scott Key. The unique irony of Howard's imprisonment is that he was imprisoned in Fort McHenry. It was this Fort that was being attacked by the British when Howard's grandfather wrote 'The Star-Spangled Banner.' Lincoln's illegal actions herein noted do not even begin to sound the depth of Lincoln's un-Constitutional activities. Furthermore, Lincoln and the Republican Party's association with radical socialists, communists, Marxists, and other "one nation indivisible" big government advocates, could fill a book—as a matter of fact, it does. One should always remember that communists, socialists, nazis, and fascists have a long-standing love affair with "one nation indivisible" government.

Lincoln proclaimed that those who believed in secession were "disloyal." Yet, President Thomas Jefferson of Virginia and President John Quincy Adams of Massachusetts both advocated secession rather than the use of force to keep the Union together. Every U.S. President before Lincoln recognized the states as sovereign and the Constitution as a document of limited government formed by a compact among the sovereign states. Lincoln, elected with only 39% of the popular vote, proclaimed that the Union created the states and therefore the Federal government was sovereign and not the states. This flimsy assertion by Lincoln was the basis for declaring that the Southern States were in rebellion against the Federal government. There is abundant evidence of the right of "we the people" of a sovereign state to withdraw its delegated rights, i.e., secede, and to "institute new Government...as to them shall seem most likely to affect their Safety and Happiness." This previous statement is drawn directly from America's most fundamental document, the Declaration of Independence, a document which also clearly states that men have the unalienable right to "alter or abolish" any government that does not protect their "Safety and Happiness." As has been stated many times, the South was Right in 1860 because America was Right in 1776—something a Yankee-educated, neo-con will not acknowledge.

When I first heard Watters make his ridiculous statement about Lincoln being kicked off Southern State ballots, I quickly texted his program the following message: "Lincoln, who won with only 39% of the vote, was not thrown off Southern state's ballots. The GOP did not have any elected officials in those states, the party did not exist there. Stop sounding like liberals when talking about the South." Of course, he did not acknowledge my text. You can text Watters at this number: 929-286-7479 and ask him why he will not give the South a chance to defend itself against his and neo-Marxist attacks. Mr. Watters, Southerners follow the wisdom of Patrick Henry: "The first thing I have at heart is American *liberty*, the second thing is American *union*." For Southerners, then and now, liberty always trumps government.

Deo Vindice.

Addendum II

SUGGESTED READING

THE FOLLOWING LIST will provide the reader with a more thorough understanding of the causes and consequences of the War for Southern Independence. This is only a partial list of quality works that provide the "rest of the story" about Southern history.

1. *The South Was Right!* A Best-Selling book which has sold over 150,000 copies and has become a standard for those seeking the complete history of the War and its consequences. Well documented to primary sources. Kennedy & Kennedy, 3rd edition, Shotwell Publishing, Columbia SC.

2. *It Wasn't About Slavery,* Dr. Samuel Mitcham, professor of history, provides critical information to destroy the woke neo-Marxist lie that the South fought the War to promote and protect slavery. Samuel W. Mitcham, Jr., Regnery History, Washington, DC.

3. *Punished with Poverty,* because of Yankee invasion and conquest, the rich and healthy South has been reduced to poverty and disease. Rather than ending slavery, the War created sharecroppers, both black and white, who were little more than economic slaves. Kennedy & Kennedy, Shotwell Publishing, Columbia, SC.

4. *The Real Lincoln,* Dr. Thomas DiLorenzo has given America one of the most eye-opening accounts of the tyrant, Abraham Lincoln. A follow-up book by DiLorenzo, *Lincoln Unmasked,* completes the destruction of the Lincoln icon. Thomas J. DiLorenzo, Prima Publishing, Roseville, CA.

5. *Lincoln, Marx, and the GOP,* shocking analysis of Lincoln and the GOP's connection with radical socialists, Marx and Engels, and Hitler. Kennedy and Benson, Shotwell Publishing, Columbia, SC.

6. *Confederate Myth-Buster,* A summary of the Southern views on secession, slavery, and the War. In a question-and-answer format, questions and answers taken for the hundreds of interviews done by the author. W. D. Kennedy, Scuppernong Press, Wake Forest, NC.

7. *Reconstruction: Destroying the Republic-Creating an Empire,* a bold and honest appraisal of the Reconstruction era that extends to the present age. Ron Kennedy, Shotwell Publishing, Columbia, SC.

ABOUT THE AUTHOR

WALTER D. (DONNIE) KENNEDY is a life member of the Sons of Confederate Veterans and is best known as the author and co-author of several pro-South books. The most notable book the Kennedy Twins have written is 'The South Was Right' which has sold over 150,000 copies.

Many in the media have noted the Kennedy Twins advocacy of limited government, that is, real States' Rights, which have led to several interviews and TV appearances. The Kennedy Twins have been interviewed by numerous local and national talk radio shows including Col. Oliver North's radio show, Alan Comes radio show, Bill Maher's show Politically Incorrect, BBC, and French National TV.

From 2018 to July of 2022 Donnie served as Chief of Heritage Operations and Ron Kennedy as Deputy Chief of Heritage Promotions for the Sons of Confederate Veterans (SCV). In July of 2022 Donnie was elected Lt. Commander-in-Chief of the SCV and Ron was appointed as the Chief of Heritage Operations for the SCV. Both have served as Commander of the Louisiana Division SCV. They have received special recognition awards from the SCV's Commander-in-Chief, including the Robert E. Lee Medal and (Donnie) the Jefferson Davis Medal. Both have been awarded the Jefferson Davis Historical Gold Medal from the United Daughters of the Confederacy and numerous other awards from various Southern Heritage organizations.

MORE BY THE KENNEDY TWINS

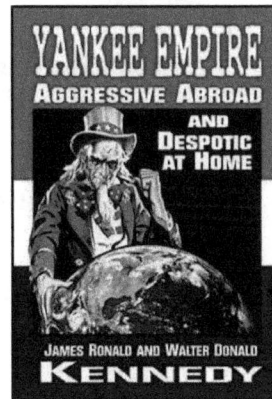

OVER 90 TITLES FOR YOU TO ENJOY

SHOTWELLPUBLISHING.COM

JEFFERY ADDICOTT
Union Terror: Debunking the False Justifications for Union Terror

Trampling Union Terror: Riders of the Second Alabama Cavalry

MARK ATKINS
Women in Combat: Feminism Goes to War

JOYCE BENNETT
Maryland, My Maryland: The Cultural Cleansing of a Small Southern State

GARRY BOWERS
Slavery and The Civil War: What Your History Teacher Didn't Tell You

Dixie Days: Reminiscences Of a Southern Boyhood

JERRY BREWER
Dismantling the Republic

ANDREW P. CALHOUN
My Own Darling Wife: Letters From A Confederate Volunteer

JOHN CHODES
Segregation: Federal Policy or Racism?

Washington's KKK: The Union League During Southern Reconstruction

WALTER BRIAN CISCO
War Crimes Against Southern Civilians

DAVID T. CRUM
Stonewall Jackson: Saved by Providence

JOHN DEVANNY
Continuities: The South in a Time of Revolution

Lincoln's Continuing Revolution: Essays of M.E. Bradford and Thomas H. Landess

JOSHUA DOGGRELL
Doxed: The Political Lynching of a Southern Cop

JAMES C. EDWARDS
What Really Happened?: Quantrill's Raid On Lawrence, Kansas

TED EHMANN
Boom & Bust In Bone Valley: Florida's Phosphate Mining History 1886-2021

JOHN AVERY EMISON
The Deep State Assassination of Martin Luther King Jr.

DON GORDON
Snowball's Chance: My Kidneys Failed, My Wife Left Me & My Dog Died...

JOHN R. GRAHAM
Constitutional History of Secession

PAUL C. GRAHAM
Confederaphobia

When The Yankees Come: Former Carolina Slaves Remember

Nonsense on Stilts: The Gettysburg Address & Lincoln's Imaginary Nation

JOE D. HAINES
The Diary of Col. John Henry Stover Funk of the Stonewall Brigade, 1861-1862

Green Altar (Literary Imprint)

CATHARINE BROSMAN
*An Aesthetic Education
and Other Stories (2nd Ed)*

Chained Tree, Chained Owls: Poems

Aerosols and Other Poems

Partial Memoirs

RANDALL IVEY
*A New England Romance:
And Other Southern Stories*

The Gift of Gab

SUZANNE JOHNSON
Maxcy Gregg's Sporting Journals 1842-1858

JAMES E. KIBLER, JR.
Tiller : Claybank County Series, Vol. 4

The Gentler Gamester

*In the Deep Heart's Core: Poems of Tribute and
Remembrance (forthcoming)*

THOMAS MOORE
*A Fatal Mercy:
The Man Who Lost The Civil War*

PERRIN LOVETT
The Substitute, Tom Ironsides 1

KAREN STOKES
Belles

Carolina Twilight

Honor in the Dust

The Immortals

The Soldier's Ghost: A Tale of Charleston

WILLIAM THOMAS
*Runaway Haley:
An Imagined Family Saga*

*The Field of Justice: Moonshine
and Murder in North Georgia*

CLYDE N. WILSON
*Southern Poets and Poems, 1606-1860:
The Land They Loved, Volume 1*

*Confederate Poets and Poems, Vol1
The Land They Loved, Volume II*

Gold-Bug
(Mystery & Suspense Imprint)

BRANDI PERRY
Splintered: A New Orleans Tale

MARTIN WILSON
To Jekyll and Hide

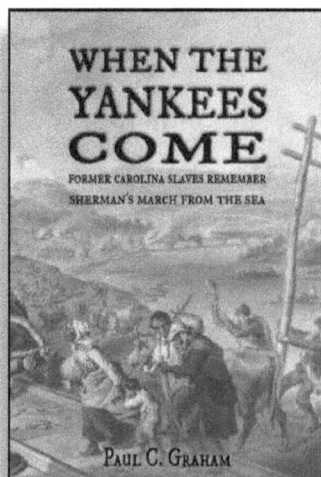

www.ingramcontent.com/pod-product-compliance
Lightning Source LLC
Chambersburg PA
CBHW072148090426
42739CB00013B/3316